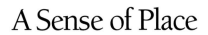

A Sense of Place

DAVID PLOWDEN

A
Sense of Place

Foreword by David Crosson

Published by the State Historical Society of Iowa
in association with
W.W. Norton & Company

New York / London

This publication was funded in part
by a grant from the State Historical Society, Inc., Iowa City.
Funding for the photographs was provided in part by
an Exemplary Award to the Iowa Humanities Board from
the National Endowment for the Humanities.

The text of this book is composed in ITC Berkeley Old Style, Medium.
Composition by Vladimir Art Studio
Manufacturing by Garner Printing.
Book design by Hugh O'Neill.

First Edition

Library of Congress Cataloging-in-Publication Data
Plowden, David.
A sense of place / David Plowden : foreword by David Crosson. — 1st ed.
p.   cm.
1. Iowa — Description and travel — 1981– —Views.
2. Landscape — Iowa — Pictorial works. I. Title.
F622. P58 1988

917.7 — dc19   88–22552

ISBN 0-393-02618-3

W.W. Norton & Company, Inc., 500 Fifth Avenue, New York, N.Y. 10110
W.W. Norton & Company Ltd., 37 Great Russell Street, London WC1B 3NU

1 2 3 4 5 6 7 8 9 0

To Sandra — who taught me what
a sense of place means

Foreword

Truth is a matter of the imagination.
— Ursula K. Le Guin,
The Left Hand of Darkness

This is not a book about Iowa, at least not just about Iowa. This is a book about cultural symbolism, about the evolution and physical manifestations of a value system and the culture that those values both created and maintain. It is a book about fact and folklore, reality and mythology. It is about what we are, what we were, and what we are becoming.

Every four years since 1972 America has rediscovered Iowa, nestled somewhere out among those square states in the middle of the country. Is it Iowa or Idaho or Ohio? Do Iowans raise potatoes or buckeyes or corn? Little matter. It is out there when we need it, when we want to recall our values or at least what we would like our values to be. Like Brigadoon, Iowa quadrennially rises in the mists of the broad valley between the Alleghenies and the Rockies. Then it is gone, and the life of the nation can continue as before.

During these brief moments in the spotlight Iowa becomes both more and less than it really is. It is transformed into a psychological landmark in a national search for self-identity, at the same time both representative and unique, anachronistic and contemporary, timely and timeless. Iowa, and to some degree the entire Midwest, become a living remnant of a lost ideal.

Both the ideal and its symbolic manifestations are as old as the Republic itself. The virtues of agrarian democracy were first understood and expressed by that most cosmopolitan of Americans Thomas Jefferson. The image of a nation of independent farmer-citizens serviced by a sprinkling of agriculturally based support communities has been nurtured throughout the occupations of vast territories. It has created its own literature, its own art, and its own region: the Midwest. In Jay Norwood ("Ding") Darling it even found its own Pulitzer Prizewinning cartoonist and its own caricatured icon, "Farmer John." Indeed, the image of the (supposedly) independent midwestern farmer has risen to the level of national folklore, with a life and function entirely its own.

There is no question that the family farm — as often as not these days the family corporation — remains one of the most sacred symbols of American values. A year after Iowa State

University published the results of a conference entitled "Is There a Moral Imperative to Save the Family Farm?" the American Association for State and Local History sponsored a national seminar for museum professionals in Des Moines called "Interpreting Rural America." That same year, however, a historian of American land policy, Dr. John Opie, seriously challenged both the accuracy and the usefulness of the Jeffersonian model. Opie argues that "the inability of today's family farmers to save themselves is based in large part on their continued dedication to the myth that they are the bulwark of private enterprise because they still work their own property." Yet the myth persists.

People cling to symbols long after economic and social changes have made them obsolete. Sometimes societal commitment to symbols provides badly needed stability during times of upheaval and dislocation. At least as often, strong symbol identifications prevent people from realizing the nature of the change that is already upon them.

It is particularly ironic that at the very time that the state is being idealized as a paradigm of Jeffersonian democracy, Iowa is in danger of losing its own most important physical symbols in the farmstead and the small town. Iowans, it seems, have not been as concerned with their own iconography as has the rest of the country. They have been too busy trying to stay "modern." Square Victorian farmhouses have given way to split-levels, barns have become almost obsolete, and the adornment and craftsmanship of small-town storefronts have been hidden by "Z-brick."

If the symbols are disappearing, are the values they represent fading, too? Is Jeffersonian America gone? Did it ever exist? Or did the Jeffersonian ideal simply tumble like a dislodged cornice into the historical salvage heap of outdated virtues? Perhaps it is still there, just hidden behind new makeup. These are the questions this book attempts to raise. The answers are left to you.

Photography is the perfect medium for documenting the changing nature of cultural symbolism. Symbols are by nature visual, and they require a visual method of documentation. To this end photography is the purest form of document. By freezing an instant of time, the photographic image contains everything that is known about its subject at that particular moment. Neither sage nor scholar is required to reveal or interpret the hidden mysteries and truths of a photograph. By carefully examining the photographic document, you can be your own historian.

On the other hand, creation of the photographic image employs the subjective (and very personal) vision of the photographer as artist. Historians often confuse facts with truth. Don Quixote's observation that facts are the enemies of truth may be overstated, but the collection and analysis of data often obfuscate the truth. Historical veracity demands careful attention to factual documentation, but artistic inspiration is required to discover — and certainly to express — the truths that the facts, left to themselves, may conceal.

This was the task presented to David Plowden: to document Iowa's rural and small-town landscape through expression of his own artistic vision. We asked him to be both artist and historian, a difficult task for anyone. The assignment was made even more difficult in that the subject matter — rural America — has assumed a symbolic life of its own. We were asking Plowden to document the changing face of an American mythology, to photograph the image of an image. He has succeeded magnificently.

In these photographs David Plowden has not only documented the disappearing face of the rural landscape but also captured the human values that created that landscape and that will long endure after the forms themselves are gone. He has created a new iconography. The images transcend form and function to provide living testimony to the strength and endurance of the values they embody. Thomas Jefferson would be pleased.

From earth to farm to town to farm to earth again. God gives, but humans must improve. The land is there, but it must be tilled. Once crops are produced, they must go to market, so section roads uniting farms run into asphalt roads to the local market and interstate highways to larger markets still. Farmers built those big foursquare houses in the last century as soon as they could afford them. The lowslung ranch houses of the past three decades are their logical successors. And it is only a small step, after all, from a wooden false storefront to a pseudobrick facade. Both aspire to be something they are not. The aspirations are the same; only their expressions have changed.

Plowden's most singular achievement is in creating a sense of loss, perhaps more accurately, of losing, while avoiding the aura of hopelessness. Look in the faces of John Haggerty and Herman Schiller and Don Frizzel. There is no desperation in their faces. And there is no sense of hopelessness in Art and Ione Johnson or Bill Haroff or Carl Lee. Buildings may fall, farmsteads may be consumed, and towns may boom only to disappear. It has always been so. But the land is still young, and the human spirit will persevere.

In the end the image with which we are left is one of hope. This is the ultimate truth revealed by David Plowden the artist and documented by David Plowden the historian. It is a hope that, in the dramatically changing landscape, where nothing that matters really changes, America might again rediscover its own "sense of place." Then we might again find an appropriate place for those who continue to live the Jeffersonian dream.

This book is a product of the most ambitious collaborative effort in the history of the State Historical Society of Iowa. The photographs were jointly contracted by the Historical Society and the Iowa Humanities Board. A National Endowment for the Humanities Exemplary Award to the Iowa Humanities Board helped fund both the photography and a state traveling exhibition of fifty prints.

The exhibition of all these photographs in the State Historical Museum in Des Moines, from December 1988 through February 1989, was made possible through the generous continuing support of the Iowa General Assembly and Governor Terry E. Branstad. Publication of this book, the first joint venture between the State Historical Society of Iowa and a major commercial publishing house, was underwritten in part by a grant from the State Historical Society, Inc., of Iowa City.

Several people deserve special recognition. Christie Dailey, representing the State Historical Society, and Jim Mairs, of W. W. Norton & Company, combined their editorial skills in a model working relationship. As president of the State Historical Society, Inc., Marion Neely invested confidence in the project at a critical time. I owe a great debt of gratitude to John Bennett, of the University of Iowa, for introducing me to David Plowden in 1986. And Iowa Humanities Board Executive Director Donald Drake deserves credit for making this cooperative project a significant part of his 1988 state program and for never losing faith.

Most of all, I would like to thank the author-artist-historian David Plowden. Few people combine his level of scholarly integrity with such artistic vision. Our physical, intellectual, and creative travels together over the past two years will long be treasured. I am proud to call him a colleague. Iowa is fortunate to call him a friend.

DAVID CROSSON, administrator,
State Historical Society of Iowa

Acknowledgments

This book is the culmination of a six-year association with Iowa, which I look upon as one of the most productive and rewarding periods in my life. During the course of that time I came to know many Iowans who offered to help a stranger with a camera, who was trying to photograph their world and who took much interest in what I was doing. I was welcomed by many who invited me into their homes. I came to know farmers along with those who owned stores along Main Street and others who worked in grain elevators — and bankers, too. While I would not presume to say that I know Iowa, I can say, after having been in almost all ninety-nine counties, that I grew to love it.

The scope of this project makes it impossible for me to name all those who helped in one way or another to bring it to fruition. To try to do so would inevitably mean that I would forget the names of some who deserve to be mentioned. I hope it will be understood, therefore, that my thanks and appreciation to all who were involved are implicit. I owe each and every one the deepest debt of gratitude.

There are a few, however, without whose contribution it would have been impossible to have made these pictures. I would like to thank, most particularly, David Crosson, administrator of the State Historical Society of Iowa, without whose enthusiasm and faith this project would have never come to pass. When we were talking about how to turn this idea into a reality he said: "There are some things which we must find a way of making happen. Trust me and we will." I did, and now it is my turn to thank him for trusting me. In the course of our callaboration I feel that we have become friends. I would like to thank as well the State Historical Society of Iowa itself, for the generous support which it has provided. To Donald Drake, executive director of the Iowa Humanities Board, also go a full measure of credit and many thanks for his staunch support throughout this project. It was nice to discover a fellow Red Sox fan as well. I should also like to thank the Iowa Humanities Board for its substantial contribution.

There are many others, as I said, to thank, but I owe a special debt of gratitude to the following: first, to all of my students at the University of Iowa who were so helpful over the course of this project; to my dear friend and colleague Drake Hokanson, who provided me with better advice and insight than almost anyone else I know; and to John Bennett, assistant professor at the School of Journalism at the University of Iowa, in whose department I had the pleasure of teaching for five years. He not only encouraged me to undertake this project but introduced me to those who would make it possible. To Christie Dailey, head of publications for the Iowa State Historical Society, and to Jim Mairs of W. W. Norton & Company, my editors on this book, thank you, not only for helping me express my ideas but for having such patience with my stubbornness. Once again, many thanks to Hugh O'Neill for being so appreciative of my photographs and for designing such a beautiful book around them. In the end, it was Sandra, my wife, although she would emphatically deny that she had any role in this project, who gave the most steadfast support of all.

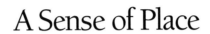

A Sense of Place

It was a raw February afternoon, the kind of day that feels as if it is going to snow but doesn't. The sky was iron gray. It was bleak and windy. The wind always blows in Iowa except in the dead heat of summer, when it is so still you can hear the corn growing. I was on my way to a farm west of Victor to explore the possibilities of making some photographs. I already had an entrée, so I didn't have to explain what I was doing from scratch. My friend Steve at the feed store in town, who was always on the lookout for places for me to photograph, had called to say I was coming.

I drove into the driveway past the front of the house and stopped opposite the kitchen door. Several cats skittered away under a shed, and the ubiquitous farm dog started barking. I rolled down the window and started saying a few soothing words, trying to convey a message of friendliness. But this old fellow seemed more bluff than threat. Besides, I saw the figure of a man appear behind the door. He opened it, said a few good-natured gruff words to the dog, and beckoned to me to come inside.

The farm itself was a century farm, a distinction which meant it had been in the same family for at least 100 years, a long time in this part of the world. Iowa itself was admitted to the Union only 142 years ago, ancient history in American terms. The buildings had a comfortable well-worn look. But it was obvious that they now were not used as much as they once had been. The farm was typical, almost indistinguishable from a thousand others dotted across the Iowa landscape. It was predominantly an assortment of white frame buildings whose configuration had been determined by their use: a corncrib; a few silos of disparate height and vintage; a machine shed and shop; a row of corrugated steel Butler storage bins; a long Morton building which was probably used to house hogs; and the common cluster of nondescript sheds in the background. Of course, there was the usual assortment of machinery in various states of repair and usefulness lying about. It seems that farmers everywhere never throw away anything in case some part of it might possibly be of use someday. All this was clustered around the centerpiece, a huge, cavernous barn, left over from another era. Like most farms in this part of the world, its configuration was reminiscent of a medieval castle. Here they are strongholds against the elements, which are often every bit as threatening as a conquering army.

I hardly had a chance to take off my coat and my boots on the enclosed porch before I was ushered through another door into the warmth of the kitchen. Although nobody ever told me to do so, it is a cardinal rule in a place where black dirt and pig and cow manure and chemicals are predominant that one never wears boots in the house. Once inside, I was greeted by the man's wife and the smell of freshly baked tollhouse cookies, which she had quite obviously prepared for my arrival. We made our introductions. The coffeepot was full, and she asked me to sit down at a big round table in the middle of the room. There were already three places set, and in the center was a plate piled high with the cookies.

Aside from being warm and cozy, the kitchen — in fact, the whole interior of the house — belied its exterior appearance. I found this to be the case in most of the Iowa farmhouses I visited. Many had been renovated and looked as modern and up-to-date as any house in a suburban development. A surprising number of the old white foursquare frame farmhouses, long synonymous with this part of the world, have been forsaken by their owners in favor of those garden-variety tract houses which are proliferating in the American countryside. It's a matter not only of being in step with the times and of the pride which is reflected in Iowa's pristine fields but of pure practicality as well. Old houses are drafty, costly to heat and keep in good repair. Save for perhaps those in the Amish country, the "traditional" kitchens that one imagines will be found on every farmstead exist only in Hollywood's version of how things should be. Everywhere else they are becoming as rare as the old Farmall "M" tractors.

No matter. The kitchen, whatever its appearance, is the heart and soul of every farmhouse. The centerpiece is always a large and usually round wooden table like the one at which we were sitting. Aside from being a place to eat, the table serves another and equally important function. It is where all major decisions are made, and all family matters decided. Essentially the kitchen is a working space geared to the production of meals for hungry men and children. Although that was no longer the case here, the predominance of new and almost new Maytag and General Electric appliances placed at strategic intervals around the room spoke plainly enough. This kitchen was far from defunct. Here, as in most, there was an oversize freezer large enough, it would have seemed, to have taken this couple several years to consume its contents. Tucked under a counter there was also, I noticed, a trash compactor, the sight of which surprised me at first, but I realized it was not a luxury as it might have been in suburbia. Out here there is no twice-weekly garbage pickup, and tight little packages are a lot easier to cart to the dump than overloaded garbage cans.

But the nature of a kitchen is not purely utilitarian. There are always many things that reflect the taste and personality of the family, little clues here and there. This one was no exception. On the wall next to the stove hung a miniature iron skillet and an array of potholders, souvenirs collected from many places, which were obviously too precious to use. On the opposite wall in a place of prominence was a Regulator clock, and although it was a reproduction, its ticking sounded just the same way as those I remember from my childhood. Carefully arranged on top of a cabinet was a group of family pictures: their children, their grandchildren, and two older couples, no doubt my hosts' parents. On the refrigerator door were several magnets, one in the shape of a heart, another of an ear of corn. Next to the clock was a calendar, which like so many others in this flat part of the world, depicted a mountain scene with a clear, rushing trout stream flowing through the foreground. At the back of one of the spotlessly clean countertops was a row of canisters. Laid out in front of these were all the utensils necessary for baking a pie, the making of which had been postponed, perhaps in favor of the cookies. There were other essentials, too. A flyswatter hung from a hook on the wall within easy reach of whoever sat in the chair next to the window. There was a mud mat just inside the door lest for some reason you forgot to remove your boots on the porch. Perhaps most crucial of all, a coffeemaker that was never empty sat on the counter nearest the table.

Through the doorway past the stove was the rest of the house, which, compared with the kitchen, appeared to be almost an afterthought. The front parlor at the end of the hall with its deep wall-to-wall carpet and matching set of couch and chairs seemed eerily unused despite the prominence of an enormous oaken TV console.

My eye fell upon the window, and I realized that the light was waning and that if I wanted to make any photographs today, I had better start soon. I was torn. The warmth of the kitchen was so inviting. Outside, the sky looked bleaker than ever. Although I had come here this afternoon specifically to photograph, the idea of donning my huge parka and boots again and then unpacking all my equipment from the car and setting forth in the cold to look for pictures didn't seem in the least appealing. That plate of still-warm cookies pushed in my direction and the full cup of steaming coffee did the trick. There would be other, better times to photograph.

Years ago I learned never just to arrive at someone's home, particularly a farm, without taking time to explain exactly what I was doing. In the winter, when there's not that much going on anyway, explanations have a nice way of turning out to be real visits, where the coffee cups are never empty and time doesn't seem to matter. It is a different story at harvest or planting time.

For a while we talked about the cold, and then we talked about children; they had three, and I told them about my four and that I was newly a grandfather. The latter revelation seemed to cement our relationship a little, for they were old hands in that role, which they obviously relished.

"Steve said you were making a book on Iowa," she said, refilling my cup.

"Yes," I said, and then I started to explain what I was doing and that the reason I was here was that I wanted to photograph their farm.

"It's not what it used to be. We're sort of semiretired now," he said, adding, "I'll be seventy-four my next birthday."

Then he went on to explain that their son-in-law, "who lived just south of town," came over twice a day to help with the chores. They still had a few hogs, about twenty steers, and a similar number of sheep.

He began to reminisce about how it had been, obviously savoring the picture he was seeing in his mind's eye. He told me that they used to milk between forty and fifty head every day, twice a day. We talked. Rather, he talked, and I listened, asking a few questions here and there, trying to visualize for myself what those mostly cold and empty barns had been like when they were filled with warm, breathing animals, the smell of fresh manure, and the voices of men. We talked about the land and then about the future, about what he thought was going to happen. Like so many others I had talked to, he felt that a lot of farmers had got into trouble by buying too much land and too much new machinery when prices were high, but that those who had been more careful, more conservative, "farmed well" as he put it, would survive. Crisis was nothing new. This was not the first and would certainly not be the last. Adversity was obviously no stranger to him, and he seemed reassuringly fatalistic about the outlook.

"We never really had it that good anyway," he said after a pause, "so things don't seem that bad now."

For a moment none of us spoke. Then she pushed the plate of cookies in my direction again and said, "You must be from east of the river, aren't you?"

"Is it that obvious?"

"It's that eastern brogue," she said, smiling. "What brought you to Iowa?"

I could see that they were genuinely curious and perhaps a little suspicious of this stranger who had knocked on the door this blustery wintry afternoon to ask if he could take some pictures. Under the circumstances they were certainly more than justified in trying to find out who I was and what I was doing, and I felt obliged to try to explain. I realized, too, from many years of experience in similar circumstances how easy it would be for them to misconstrue my intentions and that I must try to make it clear that I had come to Iowa not as a critic but as a friend.

As a photographer you have to accept the fact that when you have a camera in hand and especially when you are carrying and setting up a tripod, you will be regarded with suspicion, always as a creature of nefarious purpose. Because of the tripod, I am often mistaken for a surveyor. No matter what, the photographer is up to no good, a harbinger of unwanted change: The street will be widened, a sewer dug through the garden, the taxes raised....

I began by saying that I had grown up not only east of the Mississippi but east of the Hudson River as well, right in the midst of New York City and in Vermont, where most of the people I knew were far more familiar with Europe than anything west of the Hudson. To them Iowa, like most of the Midwest, was an unknown commodity, as it had been to me until I went to work for the railroad in Minnesota right after college. That was the first time I had actually lived anywhere in America except on the East Coast.

I went on to explain I had come to Iowa in 1983 to do the photographs for an article on Grundy County for *Smithsonian* magazine. The story was supposedly about corn, but in reality it was about Iowa. In fact, most of the photographs had nothing whatsoever to do with corn.

"I guess it was there that the seed for this project was planted, and I knew then that I had to find a way of coming back."

She smiled and remarked that I must have photographed many places since then.

I replied that judging by the number of miles I had driven, I must have been on every road in Iowa. But I sensed that I still hadn't satisfied their curiosity, so I went on to say that what I was attempting to give was an impression of what Iowa and rural America were like.

I thought for a moment, then said, "I suppose what I am really trying to do is to give a sense of place."

She nodded, and I went on to say that trying to deal with all ninety-nine counties was an impossibility. Instead, I had chosen a half dozen or so representative areas across the state and concentrated my efforts on those. This, I felt, was the best way to become familiar with the terrain and the people, and they with me. If I tried to cover everything, I would spend most of the time driving instead of making photographs.

He asked me why I had chosen this particular corner of the state to photograph.

"Well, that's long story," I replied. "One of my students at the university —"

"You're a teacher?"

I answered that I taught part-time in the School of Journalism at the University of Iowa and that a student in one of my classes a few years ago who came from Deep River happened to be a good friend of Steve's. "And so one thing led to another — and finally to your kitchen."

They asked more questions: whether I was doing just farms or the cities and towns as well.

"No cities," I replied, realizing full well that more than 50 percent of Iowa's population lives in urban areas and that more people are engaged in manufacturing than in farming. Then, warding off a question that I had been asked many times, I told them that I was not dealing with the rivers either. The Missouri and the Mississippi have their own distinct cultures, which are very different from the rest of Iowa. "It's the land in between, the farmland, that interests me."

Despite the fact that Middle West has been my "beat" for more than twenty years and that I have done more work here than in any other part of the world, I have always felt as if I were on a visa and that before long my "green card" would expire. I am not a native and will never be one. Over the years I have come to accept my role. Nevertheless, it is hard to explain to people who probably believe that because you are not one of them, you are not qualified to comment on their world or way of life.

Whatever the case may be, all photographers are to some degree outlanders to their subjects. A certain amount of detachment is inherent when one looks at the world through a lens, and necessary, too, in order to look at things objectively. Perspective, however, has many facets, not all of them photographic by any means.

It is possible, too, that a stranger may see attributes which may be overlooked as being unimportant by those familiar with them. It is often true that the "commonplace" aspects of a culture or a region — the places where people live and work, rather than its monuments — provide a better key to the understanding of it than any other. Ironically intimacy sometimes makes the most familiar things strangers to our consciousness. Often we overlook what regularly confronts our eyes.

Being from somewhere else often allows one to see things that are familiar to others in a different and sometimes even kinder light. Also, being a stranger doesn't necessarily mean being a critic, and looking at things from another perspective doesn't always have negative connotations. This is a delicate point which is often hard to make without giving the impression that I know more about my subjects than they do about themselves. Too often having a camera in hand gives one the feeling that one is ordained with infallible vision which will define the world for all.

Whenever I think of this, I always remember a most incisive observation about a book subtitled "A Celebration of Rural America," which I illustrated a number of years ago. It was in a review published in a newspaper in one of the towns that I had photographed and the author had visited. "They came armed with their telephoto lenses and electric typewriters," it said, "and then went back to New York to tell the world all about us."

So true. That is exactly what we had done. I spent just a week there and understood as much about that town as several of my English cousins did after they visited America. Usually they would fly to New York, then to Boston, and thence to Washington. Occasionally they would visit Vermont. One or two actually flew on to San Francisco for a day or two, before flying home to London over the Pole. A few days later a letter would arrive saying how much they had enjoyed seeing America.

I do not pretend to say that I know Iowa, but I have spent the greater part of the last five years photographing nothing else. During the course of those years most of the preconceptions I may have had about Iowa were dispelled. I did come to discover that Iowans are generally a little more sensitive to being typecast than most of us. But then so are New Yorkers, as I know first hand, and Chicagoans, who never seem able to overcome the second city syndrome. Many Iowans I have met seem overly sensitive about their "ruralness." They seem to doubt that I, the outlander, would ever think of Iowa as being anything but a land of pigs and corn and beans, in spite of the fact that I don't look at it that way in the least.

Iowans may be perceived as being rural, but they usually confound their critics. The state has the highest literacy rate of all fifty in the Union, and although I haven't found the statistics to prove it, there seem to be almost as many libraries in the state as the ubiquitous Casey's convenience stores.

I remember talking several years ago to a man who owned a very large and flourishing farm in Grundy County in the midst of some of the deepest and richest loam on earth. From where we stood amid a veritable arsenal of the latest and most powerful machines that John Deere & Company had to offer: there was nothing but prosperity in sight. I think he must have sensed my wonder, for he knew I was from another place where farming by comparison is a hardscrabble affair.

"What did you expect to find here?" he said. "Grant Wood and bib overalls?"

Who was misjudging whom? A bit of reverse preconception or prejudice perhaps. What sad commentary on how little we know about each other, I thought as I drove away.

Although I shall always be an outlander in this part of the world, I have grown to love the working farmland of the Middle West perhaps more than any other. It has always surprised me that this country and the high plains to the west, which constitute the very heart of America, are possibly the most unappreciated landscapes of all. Perhaps this is because they are essentially flat in nature, and in many cases we equate flat with boring. We have been conditioned over many generations to believe that only such places of obvious beauty as the mountains, the seacoast, and the wilderness are worthy of our attention. On the other hand, the plains and prairies, except to those who live and work there, are often regarded as a simply interminable distance to hurry across on the way to somewhere else.

Whenever I think about this attitude, I am reminded of an incident that occurred many years ago while I was crossing Kansas on a train. As I entered the dining car for lunch, I noticed that all the blinds in the car were pulled down. Once seated by the steward, I raised the one on my window and began to look out on the immensity of the flatlands, so different from the countryside I called home. No sooner had I made the move than the steward reappeared, reached over, and, pulling the blind down again, insisted, "There's nothing out there to look at, son."

Perhaps not to his eyes, but certainly to mine. I raised the blind once more and have never lowered it since.

For many years I have wanted to make a book about rural America, most especially the middle western working farmland which Iowa exemplifies so beautifully. I wanted to photograph not only the land and the towns, the farms and the farmers but also the relationships that form the fabric of that society. In other words, I wanted to find a way of photographing those cultural values and attitudes toward the land which are embodied in the principles of Jeffersonian democracy. These, I believe, lie at the root of American philosophy. To have a belief is one thing; to be able to photograph it is quite another. Perhaps this was an impossibility. Nonetheless, I had to try, and Iowa seemed the best place.

It was never my intention to study the problems of our agricultural economy or to emphasize the evidence of despair. Anyone who has been to Iowa recently understands that much of the traditional way of life is changing. That was the reason I began making these photographs in the first place, but my focus was on the aspects of our farming culture which are vanishing as well as those that I hope will endure.

To most of the world Iowa is perceived of as a land of corn and pigs. Beans, although they are the state's second-largest cash crop, have never been synonymous with its image. But corn is another matter altogether. It is in a class by itself, 100 percent American, our indigenous grain, and Iowa produces more of it than any other state. Despite this, I find Iowa to be much more beautiful when the corn isn't tall, especially in the spring and fall, when one can see the land itself. So it was to the land and the farmsteads that float, miragelike upon its surface, that I turned to at first.

But there are many facets to Iowa besides the obvious. It would be impossible, for instance, to photograph Iowa, or the North American midlands, without grain elevators. They are the most prominent structures in the landscape. I suppose that because of my having lived in New York for so many years, I see the grain elevator as a form of indigenous skyscraper rising above the prairie, heralding even the smallest hamlet as a place of consequence. I am not alone in my admiration. It is told that H. H. Richardson, the great nineteenth-century architect, who was as imposing a figure as the buildings he designed, said that one of the things he most wanted to design was a grain elevator.

It would be remiss, too, to depict Iowa without its churches, especially those on some remote crossroads, where there are but single Sunday services. During the rest of the week, I found, the doors were rarely locked either—a major difference between rural culture and urban. Only recently have people begun to find it necessary to take refuge behind locks, an unfortunate sign of the changing times.

Churches, farms, grain elevators, and the towns clustered at their feet are the singular iconography of mankind's presence on Iowa's landscape.

Whatever else, the most important ingredient of all is the people who make things work. They are the enduring heroes of an ever-changing world. Perhaps because I felt this way, I found photographing the people I met in Iowa the greatest challenge of all.

It is one thing to photograph somebody at work, quite another to make a portrait of the same person at home. For instance, I felt that it was entirely in order for me to ask permission of my hosts this afternoon to photograph their farm, but that we would have to know each other longer before I should expect to be allowed to make photographs of them. To me the taking of someone's picture is not a right. It is part of a dialogue, a trust established between photographer and subject, which often takes a long time to achieve. The more I photograph, the more respect I have for the belief held by the Amish, the American Indians, and others that by taking someone's picture, you steal part of his or her soul.

Very early in the project I discovered it was hard enough to get anyone to pose for a portrait, but it was virtually impossible to get a woman to do so unless her husband was with her.

I once asked a farmer whom I had come to know quite well during the course of several months if I could take his picture. It was October, and he was changing heads on his combine parked by the machine shed. "Maybe next week" was his reply. "The weather's right for beans." Next week turned out to be right for something else, certainly not for picture taking. Finally, three weeks later, when the harvest was winding down, I decided to try again. This time I telephoned first before driving over endless miles of dusty section roads only to be told once again that "this week" was the wrong time. His wife answered. I asked if it might be all right to come out that day. She said she'd ask him. She put the telephone down, and I heard her calling to her husband in a loud voice, "It's that photographer again. He wants to take your picture today." In the distance I heard an emphatic no. Then her voice again: "He says no."

Although I can be pretty persistent when I'm on the trail of a photograph, I felt there was no use in pursuing the matter further. I said that I was disappointed, that I really would have liked to have him in the book, and her as well, but, of course, I realized how busy he was—all perfectly true. Just as I was about to say good-bye, she broke in: "Tell you what, if you're here at one o'clock, I'll make sure he's here, too."

At the appointed hour I knocked on their kitchen door. He was there as promised, freshly shaven, in a shirt straight out of the dryer, with his hair obviously just combed.

"How long's this going to take?" he said.

"About five minutes."

"OK, that's what you've got."

I got his picture and, what was even nicer, both of them together. She, too, had dressed for the occasion much as if she were going to the photographic studio on Main Street for a sitting.

Children, on the other hand, I have found always more than willing to be photographed, usually asking first, "Hey, mister, take my picture." And if you don't, they follow you until you do. In one town two young boys on bicycles showed up whenever I stopped to set up. Finally I asked them what they were up to. They replied that they were the only kids in town, and as they had seen me photographing everything else, why shouldn't I take their picture, too? In another place the fact that one little girl on her bicycle stopped to ask what I was doing became the key that unlocked a whole treasure trove of photographs. Children always know what's important and what's going on, and if you have the sense to listen to them, so will you.

Trying to photograph something as elusive as a whole culture is very different from recording an event, such as a wedding or a basketball game. Even in the most straightforward circumstances I have found that 90 percent of the time photography is the art of trying to make pictures out of subjects that don't lend themselves easily to visual interpretation. The fact that I found Iowa very difficult to photograph doesn't mean that it is an uninteresting place. Quite the contrary; it just takes a long time to let itself be revealed. You have to dig deeper to find the mother lode than with many less challenging places.

Some subjects—steam engines, bridges, steel mills—are so graphic that they almost take their own photographs, but the essence of Iowa is not easily revealed in visual terms. Its landscape is not inherently dramatic, and photographing it is a constant process of searching. The smallest variation in the light, a shadow, the merest undulation of a field, a fence post next to the road, or a telephone pole in the distance becomes a major event in the visual context. The relationship of near and far objects becomes a major photographic consideration. Iowa made me look as I never had before. Its nature is as elusive as the wary trout, and photographing it reminds me very much of fly fishing. One has to learn to read the river, to be aware of the most subtle clues in the pattern of its currents, and to decipher their meaning.

I thought of a remark a friend of mine had made at the end of a very long day of guiding me around his part of the state. As we drove home, he admitted that although he had been watching me closely all day, he had a hard time seeing what I was so excited about every time we stopped to make a photograph.

"You know," he said, "after seeing you working, I think those West Coast photographers have an easier time of it."

I asked him why.

"Because I don't think they have to look so hard to find a picture. It must be easier to photograph the mountains."

I replied that I appreciated what he meant, that it wasn't easy, but I assured him that photographing the mountains had its share of problems, too, and that I wouldn't have a clue to how to cope with them.

More than any other place I know Iowa's landscape has been delineated by the grid pattern established by the Ordinance of 1785. This was another product of that brilliant, organized mind of Thomas Jefferson. It provided for a survey of all public lands lying north and west of the Ohio River, dividing them into townships of six square miles. These were subdivided into thirty-six sections, each of which contained 640 acres. Thus the square section became the basic unit of land measurement in the American West.

Perhaps nowhere is the right angle of the grid more evident than in Iowa. Everything is neatly squared, centered, ordered, as even the most casual glance at the map will reveal. The capital itself, Des Moines, is located virtually dead center, a pattern repeated in almost every instance with the county seats: Primghar, Sigourney, Hampton, New Hampton, Humboldt, Denison, Indianola, Tipton, Red Oak, and one actually called Centerville, to name but a few. Each is situated at the county's geographical center. In most, the courthouse is located at the center of the square around which the business section of town has been built. But this order is not confined to geography alone. A centrist philosophy seems to be at the core of almost every aspect of Iowa's culture. I venture to say it is not the imposition of the unnatural grid upon the land alone which makes this so.

In New York the seasons matter little, and weather is usually no more than a three-minute spot on the evening news. One carries an umbrella if it rains, and about once in a decade there is a blizzard which ties up the city completely for several days. But in Iowa, as in the rest of rural America, the repetitious chronology of the seasons regulates the lives of all who live there.

Perhaps, too, there is a stronger belief among those who live by the seasons and beneath the panoply of the stars that there is another, greater order that we who abide the chaos of the city do not understand nearly as well. Out here it is harder to believe that all we are, that all of the intricate, complex relationships which determine the course of nature and our lives are purely the result of happenstance.

There is also truth to the statement that Iowa is the middle ground. In size it ranks twenty-fifth out of the fifty states, twenty-ninth in population. Geographically, it is the middle of the Middle West, practically in the middle of the continent. But it is the middle ground in other ways as well. It ranks twenty-sixth among the states in personal income. Its politics mirrors that centrist philosophy again: Iowans desire to avoid the extreme in whatever they do. Historically they have eschewed the radical and the archconservative points of view, electing to steer a steady course of moderation through a world increasingly characterized by violent extremes. One senses that this moderation has endowed Iowans with an almost genetic calm, an inner determination that will enable them to endure despite adversity and myriad crises, none of which are new to them.

But Iowa has another face. One just has to experience its weather to know it is also a place of great extremes, of tornadoes, blizzards, blistering heat, and frigid days; it is a place where flood and drought can visit destruction on different parts of the state at the same time. It is a place where a gentle, cloudless morning sky can produce forty-thousand-foot-high thunderheads by midafternoon and destroy a whole crop with golf ball-size hail a half hour later. It can rain so hard in one place that you cannot see beyond the car's windshield, and it can be bone dry three sections away. Iowa is an elemental place, essentially just sky and earth, where the space in which we abide is merely an interface between the two. It is there, on the land, that one gets a first impression of overwhelming sameness. Yet Iowans speak of how varied their landscape is. It is, as I came to learn, but that variety is a matter of degree. Appreciating it is like tasting wine; one has to be a connoisseur of subleties.

Although Iowa's demeanor is essentially flat, it is not all level, as many not familiar with this part of the world believe. Gently rolling is perhaps a better phrase. In that regard it has often been compared with the ocean, and aptly so, for the land appears to heave and subside in great swells as does the sea after a storm. Iowa's topography has many variations, so that there is no one landform which can be called quintessentially Iowan. It is not Alpine by any stretch of the imagination, although a sign on the outskirts of a town in the state's northeastern corner might have you believe otherwise. "Welcome to Elgin, the Switzerland of Iowa," it proclaims.

To one from "east of the river" the scale of Iowa is wholly unlike anything Swiss. There are no confining valleys or mountain walls to constrict the view and perhaps one's aspirations as well. Nor is it an ancient place, steeped in history and molded by thousands of years of civilization. Although settled in large measure by Europeans who have striven to maintain their culture and traditions, Iowa, like Chicago, is thoroughly American in character. Its topography, too, appears to mirror that unbounded spirit of youthfulness which has been characteristically American. The sky is the limit, especially in northwestern Iowa. There one can imagine a little of how it must have been to be on the frontier, to have known that there was always plenty: more land, unlimited opportunity and challenge, and no need to conserve anything. In Buena Vista County, so aptly named, O'Brien, and even parts of Franklin and Grundy counties, more centrally situated, one senses the land beginning to stretch, as if in anticipation of the Great Plains. As on the plains, the scale is almost beyond the realm of photography to capture.

The sense of infinite space, the ever-present sky, the constant wind, and the earth itself give one the illusion that Iowa's environment is primarily the product of natural forces. That is true only if one uses the elements as a gauge. Today the Iowa landscape is as much the product of human endeavor as is Times Square. In fact, 94 percent of the state is arable.

I became particularly aware of this one spring evening as I drove along a section road in the midst of what seemed a very faraway place. At one point the urge to be free of my little tin prison became impossible to resist. Finally I stopped by the roadside, turned off the engine, and got out of the car. I walked to the brow of a hill, where I stood looking and listening, feeling the wind in my face. At first I felt as if I were in paradise or at least as if Persephone had returned once again to the world from her yearly sojourn in Hades. From everywhere came the song of the meadowlark, and the smell of freshly plowed earth hung in the air all around. It was the kind of evening that one yearns for so longingly in February but begins to believe will never come again. Everything was bathed in deep golden light from the sun, low in the western sky an hour or so from setting. The merest pebble in the road and each blade of grass appeared to be etched in boldest relief. It was that time of the day when for a precious moment the world seemed preserved in amber, suffused in an ageless calm which would be shattered if one spoke above a whisper.

But then, as almost everywhere else I've ever been, came the sound of an internal-combustion engine. A tractor growled in the distance, faintly at first, but more pronouncedly the longer I listened. Eventually, though it was never once in sight, it overwhelmed the lark's caroling. At the same time I became aware of an acrid smell in the air and realized that the bountiful harvest these fields would yield in the fall depended on chemicals as much as, or more than, on the fecundity of the soil itself. Once the spell was broken, I saw things in a different light. I realized that the land, from the edge of the road to the farthest horizon, as far as I could see, was held in the "hand of man."

Yet it was still beautiful. In spite of our folly, not all that we undertake or touch is vile. True, we have already squandered, spoiled, and poisoned too much of our inheritance since we arrived here. We came armed with the tools and intentions to possess and mold the land to our use. Too often the landscape is marked by the evidence of rapacity and greed, by a total lack of concern for the future. Unfortunately, rampant exploitation in the name of progress has been a recurring theme throughout our history.

Sometimes, however, as the evidence that evening indicated, this isn't always the case. This is the breadbasket. We had transformed the prairie into a working, useful place, not a wasteland. The tractor was not a machine of war. Against the sky it was diminutive as well, a gauge of our ephemeral grasp on things. The sound of its engine, jarring at first, was no longer menacing. It belonged now, a machine which was just as much a part of the landscape as the lark. The distant farms, like islands amid a sea of plowed fields which stretched away to infinity, seemed to indicate that here for a moment, at least, people and nature had achieved a state of equilibrium. As I turned to leave, I was filled with a sense of hope. After all, as I remembered my mythology again, was not hope the only thing that remained in Pandora's box after she had opened it?

While I drove away, I wondered if my feeling was a matter of conditioning. I reflected for a moment on what that view would have been like before the advent of the breaking plow. But I could only imagine how it was. The transformation has been so complete that today there is no place left where one can stand and contemplate what the vastness of the tallgrass prairie was like. The remnants that survive are just that. They exist as no more than artifacts and give no more clue to the prairie's true nature than arrowheads in a museum case give a picture of a tribe's culture.

Farther on, on the other side of a rise, the road dipped and crossed a stream whose silt-liden water ran coffee-colored toward the Mississippi. I stopped on the bridge and thought how much precious topsoil has been carried away to become part of the river's delta a thousand miles away. I remembered that Big Muddy's water used to run clear on its journey to the sea. I had read, too, that by some accounts half of the deepest, richest lode of topsoil on earth has been washed or blown away in a little more than the hundred years since we began turning the sod. Others say it will not be that long before it is all gone. In that light the tractor was an instrument of war, after all, in the perennial battle between civilization and nature which has been waged since the beginning of recorded time.

But there are hopeful signs. The concern for conservation has become increasingly evident lately. The ethic that we must reap the greatest yield from the land whatever the consequences for the future, which has persisted for so long, is beginning to change. Those neatly manicured fields which have been synonymous with Iowa and symbolic of the pride that goes with being a good farmer, but which at the same time allow the land to lie bare and exposed to the elements for much of the year, are not as numerous as they were a decade ago. Change is a slow process, however, particularly here. In a land of such bountiful proportions the idea that resources are not infinite is hard to grasp.

I sat there on the bridge, watching the water slide by, and thought about how the Mississippi and its tributaries form the largest drainage basin in North America, more than a third of the lower forty-eight states, the heartland in fact. It collects its waters all the way from western Pennsylvania to the continental divide; from two Canadian provinces to the Gulf of Mexico. So to be from east of the river, in that sense, means to be from the periphery of America, just a stone's throw away from Plymouth Rock.

By the time I reached the interstate just before the sun set I realized I was going to be late for dinner with friends, so I had better press on. I took one last look toward the west and realized it really didn't matter. Both time and change are relative. Despite all the transformations we have wrought, our sojourn here is tenuous at best. In the long run only the sky will remain anyway.

Symbolically the farmer may be Iowa's most heroic figure, and the plowed earth its great resource, but as the historian Joseph Wall says, "An understanding of the small town is critical to an understanding of the state....It has been the influential people in Iowa's small towns who have molded the state in their own image."

Having spent a lifetime stalking photographs on Main Street and the back streets from Maine to Oregon, I might go even further and say that small towns may well be the key to understanding rural America as a whole, both culturally and philosophically. I have also found in all those years spent driving the blue roads across the map that aside from obvious regional differences in flora and architecture, small towns are generically the same place.

I remember driving across Ohio against the wind on a hot summer day on one of my numerous trips back and forth across that part of the world. As the day wore on, I began to realize, after passing through town after town, that I was driving through my own photographs. Moreover, they all were of the same place. At one point I stopped at the edge of a town that I had never seen. "OK, Plowden," I said to myself. "Describe this place." I turned on my tape recorder and started to depict it in detail. Then I drove around town, and by Jove, everything was there just as I had seen it in my mind's eye. All the way home, all the way across the rest of Ohio and all of Indiana, until Chicago's presence began to be felt, it was true. The towns were indistinguishable from one another. And so it is in Iowa, too, on the surface at least. But as you get to know them better, you realize that like the faceless faces in a crowd, the small towns are individuals — distinguished somehow from all the rest.

One of the many Iowans I met said that he wouldn't have thought there was much to see in the towns, that there was nothing very special about them except that all had seen better days and were dying a slow death.

Although I didn't agree that all small towns were necessary in their death throes, I thought of more than a score of them across the state that I had photographed in the past five years and of how they were always in a state of flux. The one consistency was change, and if one is dealing with change, nowhere is it more obvioius than in town. Where everything is close together, the difference between old and new is easier to see. This is especially true when you look at the stores and even more so when you compare Main Street with what has happened on the outskirts of town: Casey's, Kwik Stop, Hardee's, and all those new little houses that seem to spring up overnight.

Small towns anywhere are archaeological sites. The adaptations and needs of each generation are laid down one upon the other in succession like sediments, wherein the evolution of our history may be plainly seen. As such they are among the best mirrors of our culture. This is especially apparent on Main Street, where the storefronts are constantly being done over in a never-ending quest to be up-to-date. It's rather like a dog race in which the poor creatures are deluded into chasing the electric rabbit which they never catch. Above street level, the original fabrics of the buildings usually remain unaltered, intact, a benchmark from which we may take a bearing.

The same is true inside as out. One store I discoverd, whose interior had remained virtually unchanged for three-quarters of a century, sold both buttons for high-button shoes and Reeboks. Even in stores that have had their pressed tin ceilings covered with acoustical tile, it is still possible to buy nails by the pound and Clabber Girl baking powder. Main Street was never a museum. It was always a working place, and still is. It was not ordained to be a particular way; it evolved, like an organism adapting to the needs of the times.

Certain things never change, I discovered, although their physical appearances may be drastically different from those of a generation ago. For instance, if there is nothing else in town, I found there is almost always a post office with the flag fluttering from a pole set in the sidewalk in front of it. Where there might have been several a decade ago, usually one bank remains. It is a dead town, indeed, that does not have a bank, a feed store, or a grain elevator. In most I found a café, which opens at 5:00 A.M. and closes at 2:00 in the afternoon, where if you sit sipping coffee and keep your ears open long enough, you will find out just about everything that's going on in town. Even if all the other stores are boarded up, usually one place remains purveying the basic needs of the people who live there, even if it is only a Casey's. Almost always there are a place to buy gas and, often, to my surprise, an honest garage where you can have flats fixed and where there is a real mechanic who can fix almost anything else on you car, too. Lately a video store, a beauty salon, or one of those boutiques that always reek of incense and sell Oriental geegaws at absurd prices have moved like squatters into the old stores. Rows of Atari games, too, have replaced the pool tables in most places, but as an old pool shark myself, I was happy to find that this was not always the case. There is always a bar or two. In fact, in more than one town I photographed, the bar was the only place still doing business, and, to judge from the cars always parked in front of it, a brisk one at that. There is a dearth of drugstores, but the chances are that if there is one, it will have a soda fountain, complete with a row of revolving stools, where you can get a hand-dipped ice-cream cone, where cherry Coke doesn't come out of a bottle and your shake will be made with a Hamilton Beach blender.

Aside from the grain elevator or the courthouse in a county seat, the school and its gymnasium are almost always the most prominent structures in town. Rarely in this part of the world will there be a factory or a mill, as in New England or Pennsylvania, which overshadows everything else. There are plenty of empty lots and crumbling foundations, big gaping holes along Main Street that were once stores, as if a tooth had been knocked out. Once there were depots, the nerve centers where everything and everybody came and went. Nearly all are gone today. There are hardly any trains anywhere anymore, and most of the tracks which once reached out to almost every hamlet in Iowa — to all of rural America for that matter — have been torn up. Along Railroad Avenue, down by the lumberyards and the grain elevators, often today there is a big scar where once there were tracks. Now glistening, brightly painted eighteen-wheelers come and go along the right-of-way where the local freight used to switch cars.

It is very hard to walk slowly if you've ever been a New Yorker, but if you live in a small town in Iowa, or anyplace in rural America for that matter, it is hard to walk down the street in town without stopping to talk to somebody. Here everybody knows everybody, and people call each other by their first names. Crime isn't a problem either, as I have been told over and over. It is possible to leave your car unlocked when you go shopping, knowing that nothing will be stolen when you came back.

I have often thought about the meaning of the word community and about how true it is that rural America and its small towns are places of common cultural heritage. Whenever I think about this, I begin to visualize the part of town which people call home and how it, too, is an archaeological site, albeit of a more human mien. Clues to the comparative wealth and status of its residents abound here. Much is revealed by a hundred years or more of eclectic architectural styles, by how the houses have been renovated or not, by the sizes of the garages, the lawn ornaments, and the number of satellite TV disks, by whether there is as motorcycle or a pickup — or both — in a driveway. Up here "on the hill," so to speak, on some secluded street, there was a house grander than the others, the place where the "richest man in town" once lived. Whether he was reviled for his parsimony or revered for his largess, the house today is usually a funeral parlor. Most of the streets are treelined; most of the houses, frame and anonymous in their plainness and painted white. Most are set back from the street and have verandas where people really still sit and rock in the cool of the evening, watching the passing traffic. In the fall the pungent smell of burning leaves raked into little piles is always present in the air. In summer the chorus of unseen cicadas shatters the oppressive heat of August afternoons when it is even too hot for dogs to scratch themselves. There are daffodils in the yards in spring, and on weekends or on warm evenings, men and boys often wash their cars in the driveways to the strains of country or rock blaring from transistors in the garage doorways. At Christmastime the evergreens by the front doors are festooned with strings of colored lights.

I have found from many years of exploring those back streets that if you listen, you will hear myriad familiar sounds, clues, too, to the nature of the place: a baby's cry; the voices on a TV soap opera — and occasionally a real drama as well — coming from an open window; the banter of two teenage girls pedaling by on their bicycles on their way home from school; and always, from spring to fall, the noise of at least one power lawn mower. In small towns, but never in the city, you can always hear footsteps on the sidewalk. At twelve o'clock the firehouse siren announces the noon hour is at hand and all work will be put aside for its duration. And I myself will head for the café down on Main Street.

Sometimes in town I have come across true anomalies, remnants from the past which somehow have remained unscathed, the real item, neither bogus reconstructions nor desecrated. Such a place was the general store in Cedar Bluff. When I opened the door, heard the bell tinkle, and crossed the threshold, suddenly I was ten years old again back in Cy Davis's Gen'l. Merchandise in Putney, Vermont. It was the same place, the same musty smell, nail, kegs, ornate cash register; even the boxes of Red Wing shoes were there on the shelves exactly as I remembered.

As I have for so many years, I arrived just in time. Three months after I was there, the store closed its doors forever, leaving only the mute shell of the building to join the ranks of its kind on the inexorable journey toward the limbo of decay.

The present owner and her brother, who had kept shop for nearly half a century, told me that the local distributors no longer thought it worth the trouble to drive a few miles out of the way to deliver produce. What little was there, she explained, had been ordered from a place in Kentucky which sent it by freight. That was too costly now, she explained, or perhaps, I believed, the truth of the matter was that it was simply too much effort now. Whatever the reason, she had stopped ordering and was selling only that which remained on the shelves. She figured it would last until school was out.

I looked out the kitchen window and realized that the sun was getting low. The sky looked more threatening than ever. The snow would not hold off forever. It was time to go.

My hostess got up, took a Baggie from a drawer, and put the rest of the cookies in it. "In case you get hungry," she said, handing it to me.

I thanked them both for such a lovely afternoon. I said I would be back, probably in the spring, when the weather and the light were better for making pictures. I began to take my leave slowly, for I would have liked to have stayed longer. They both followed me out to the porch and waited while I put on my boots ancd parka. As we shook hands, he said that I would always be welcome. Even if they weren't there, I could photograph anytime; if they came home and saw a little Honda with Illinois plates parked in their driveway, they would know not to worry.

I started my car and looked up to see them standing in the doorway. We waved once, and as I backed down the drive, the old dog, which had remained outside all the while, followed me, barking, until I turned onto the blacktop. A few minutes later I was back on the interstate, heading for home a world away, "east of the river."

I found my niche in the traffic and settled in for a good five hours behind the wheel with more than a hundred miles of Iowa still ahead of me before I crossed the Mississippi. As I sped east toward the night with the trucks, I realized I was back on the main trunk once again. For well more than a centrury, since the first transcontinental railroad, this has been the pathway for countless millions of Americans who have passed across Iowa on their way somewhere on the overland trails, by train, on the Lincoln Highway, on U.S. 20, and tonight on I-80. The lines of contrails in the sky far above the traffic told of another highway following the same path.

I realized, too, before the night closed in that more than ever Iowa is a state many know only at 65 mph from the interstate, but that if one slowed down enough to see it, the landscape beyond the right-of-way gives a fair sense of what it is like. To begin to understand Iowa, though, one must turn off at some interchange and endure the dust of the section roads, sit in a Main Street café, drive to a farmstead, and spend the kind of afternoon I had spent today. Above all, one needs to slow down, become absorbed, take time to read the landscape as the fisherman reads the river. It is not an easy thing to do these days, but the pace of Iowa is not in the fast lane.

Section road, Scott County, April 1986

Buena Vista County, June 1986

Grundy County, May 1983

Clinton County, March 1987

Clinton County, March 1987

Grundy County, May 1983

Cedar County, May 1985

Poweshiek County, April 1986

Poweshiek County, April 1986

Soybeans, Clay County, June 1986

Corncrib, Greene County, June 1986

Pocahontas County, June 1986

Jones County, May 1987

Herman Schiller, farmers' co-op elevator, Dike, August 1983

Corncrib, Wulff farm, Cedar County, February 1987

Corncrib, Price farm, Poweshiek County, February 1987

VanErsvelde farm, Brooklyn, June 1987

Cow barn, Wulff farm, Cedar County, February 1987

50

Cow barn, Wulff farm, Cedar County, February 1987

Machine shed, Nemec farm, Fairfax, September 1987

Goldsmith farm, Cedar County, June 1986

Cow barn, Van Olegham farm, Iowa County, June 1986

Cow barn, Van Olegham farm, Iowa County, June 1986

John Haggerty, Deep River, April 1986

Mechanicsville, Cedar County, May 1987

Price farm, Poweshiek County, February 1987

House, Deep River, April 1986

Deep River, April 1985

Marie Toomey's porch, Brooklyn, June 1987

Staircase and table, Lang home, Brooklyn, June 1987

Joanne and David Nemec, Fairfax, October 1987

Art and Ione Johnson, Peterson, June 1986

Johnson home, Peterson, June 1986

Bedroom, Hotel Brooklyn, Brooklyn, June 1987

Bathroom, Hotel Brooklyn, Brooklyn, June 1987

Schoolhouse, Monmouth, May 1987

Gymnasium, Montezuma School, Montezuma, October 1987

Cheri Ranfeld, Montezuma School, Montezuma, October 1987

Susan Cheney, Montezuma School, Montezuma, October 1987

Jayson Miller, Scotch Grove, May 1987

Kelley Bradley, Scotch Grove, May 1987

Peterson, June 1986

Dysart, June 1986

Reinbeck, August 1983

Deep River, April 1986

Deep River, April 1985

Cumberland, April 1987

Victor, May 1986

80

Brighton, June 1986

Ossian, March 1987

Bank vault, Eddyville, April 1987

Post office lobby, Hastings, April 1987

Bill Haroff, postmaster, Hastings, April 1987

Courthouse square, Albia, April 1987

Albia, April 1987

Brooklyn, June 1987

Montezuma, May 1985

Former Legion hall, Columbus Junction, October 1984

Former Masonic Lodge, Lucas, April 1987

Victor, May 1986

Victor Café, Victor, May 1986

Carl Lee, Columbus Junction, October 1984

Carl Lee's barbershop, Columbus Junction, October 1984

Olds, May 1986

Ladora, May 1985

John and Violet Van Waus, Van's clothing store, Victor, April 1986

Van's clothing store, Victor, April 1986

Van's clothing store, Victor, April 1986

General store, Cedar Bluff, February 1987

General store, Cedar Bluff, February 1987

General store, Cedar Bluff, April 1987

Royal café, Royal, June 1986

Whitworth's hardware, Victor, May 1986

Pawlak's, Victor, May 1986

Iberg's garage and DX station, Victor, June 1986

Iberg's garage and DX station, Victor, June 1986

Marion Baustian, Guernsey, April 1986

Bohstedt's feed store, Victor, May 1986

Hog feeders, Rossie, June 1986

Holland, May 1983

Prairieburg, May 1983

Johnson brothers' feed mill, Essex, April 1987

Aurelia, June 1986

Abandoned grain elevator, Ossian, March 1987

Grain elevators, Aurelia, June 1986

Bockes brothers' farm, Grundy County, August 1983

Lefebure farm, Fairfax, September 1987

Havelock, June 1986

Farmers' co-op elevator, Bradford, June 1986

Farmers' co-op elevator, Dike, October 1983

Don Frizzel, farmers' co-op elevator, Dike, August 1983

Jerry Keleher, Clarence co-op elevator, Clarence, October 1987

Dennis Lauterbach, farmers' co-op elevator, Dike, August 1983

Clarence co-op, Clarence, October 1987

Buckingham co-op, Buckingham, July 1987

Chapin, June 1986

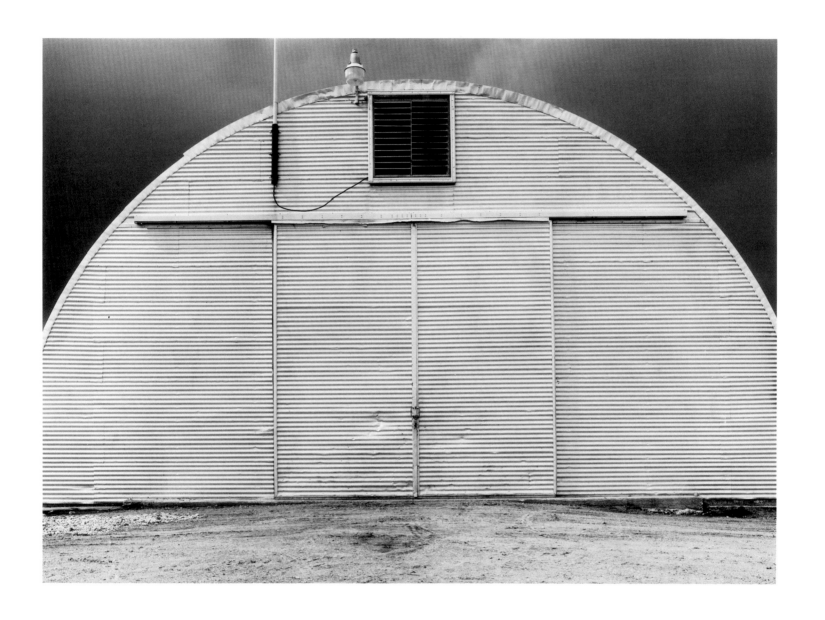

Storage bin, Holland, May 1983

Daniel Nemec, Fairfax, September 1987

Richard Bockes, Grundy County, August 1983

Ted Bohstedt, Bohstedt's elevator, Victor, May 1986

Scale, Bohstedt's elevator, Victor, June 1986

Turntable, Bohstedt's, Victor, June 1986

Westaby Grain Company, Alexander, June 1986

Armstrong Lumber Company, Dyersville, March 1987

Armstrong Lumber Company, Dyersville, March 1987

———

Methodist Episcopal Church, Winneshiek County, March 1987

Methodist Episcopal Church, Winneshiek County, March 1987

Wesley Chapel, Mills County, April 1987

Wesley Chapel, Mills County, April 1987

East Liberty Methodist Church, Mills County, April 1987

Buchanon Cemetery, Buchanon, May 1987

Rochester Cemetery, Rochester, February 1987

Iron Pratt Truss, Bluffton, March 1987

Route U.S. 30, Cedar County, April 1986

Section road, Grundy County, October 1983

Buena Vista County, June 1986

Montgomery County, April 1987

Tama County, July 1987

Jackson County, July 1983

Glen Hockemeyer, Holland, August 1983

Linn County, October 1987

———

Roger Dudden, Reinbeck, October 1983

Grundy County, October 1983

Poweshiek County, March 1986

———

Grundy County, October 1983

Cedar County, October 1987